Henley-on-Thames
in old picture postcards

by
Francis Sheppard

European Library - Zaltbommel/Netherlands MCMLXXXIII

GB   ISBN 90 288 2523 1

European Library in Zaltbommel/Netherlands publishes among other things the following series:

IN OLD PICTURE POSTCARDS *is a series of books which sets out to show what a particular place looked like and what life was like in Victorian and Edwardian times. A book about virtually every town in the United Kingdom is to be published in this series. By the end of this year about 75 different volumes will have appeared. 1,250 books have already been published devoted to the Netherlands with the title* **In oude ansichten.** *In Germany, Austria and Switzerland 500, 60 and 15 books have been published as* **In alten Ansichten;** *in France by the name* **En cartes postales anciennes** *and in Belgium as* **En cartes postales anciennes** *and/or* **In oude prentkaarten** *150 respectively 400 volumes have been published.*

For further particulars about published or forthcoming books, apply to your bookseller or direct to the publisher.

This edition has been printed and bound by Grafisch Bedrijf De Steigerpoort in Zaltbommel/Netherlands.

INTRODUCTION

About two thirds of the photographs in this book were taken during the reign of Queen Victoria, and the remainder between 1901 and about 1930. A few of them date from the 1860's, or possibly even a little earlier, and in them we are able for the first time to see Henley as it really was instead of through the eyes of a painter or engraver. We are no longer dependent on a human intermediary for our vision of the scene, and it is this feeling of direct contact which (even despite their lack of colour) often makes these earliest photographs so vivid.

The Henley of the 1850's and 1860's which they portray was no longer a prosperous place. Ever since the mid twelfth century, when the first certain references to Henley occur, the town had depended upon the river for much of its livelihood. In the middle ages and even later the upper reaches of the Thames, particularly between Wallingford and Oxford, were often not easily navigable, and part of the produce of that region, such as corn and building stone, was brought by cart to Henley for shipment to London. In the early eighteenth century three hundred cartloads of corn were sometimes sold in the market on a single day; and there was also a substantial trade in the shipment of beechwood from the Chilterns. Later in the eighteenth century Henley had also become an important centre of road communication. The roads from Maidenhead and Dorchester had been modernised by the new turnpike trusts, the very steep gradient at White Hill had been reduced in 1768 by the building of a cutting and an embankment, and the river-crossing had been much improved by the building of a wide new stone bridge in 1781-1786. In the 1830's a score of stage and mail coaches passed through the town every day, and called at one of the numerous inns.

But much of this prosperity was destroyed by the opening of the Great Western Railway in 1840. Road traffic declined so greatly that the Red Lion inn was actually closed for seven years in the 1850's, and by the 1880's the commercial traffic on the river had almost entirely withered away. In 1841 about one in ten of all the houses in the town was empty and uninhabited, and neither the establishment of the Regatta in 1839 nor even the opening of the branch railway line from Twyford in 1857 brought quick recovery.

So some of the earliest photographs reproduced here have an almost desolate air — the river and bridge empty and deserted, warehouses decaying and the streets dirty and ill-paved.

Revival seems to have begun in the 1870's, when

Duke Street was widened, the old Town Hall modernised and the first Royal Hotel built. The river, no longer a commercial artery, was beginning to be a playground, and around 1890 smart new boat-houses were displacing many of the now decrepit riverside stables and granaries. The Regatta was becoming both more popular and more fashionable, particularly after the changes made in 1886. On the southern outskirts of the town new houses were being built in the 1880's and 1890's, while in the middle the Town Hall and a number of shops had been rebuilt by the end of the Victorian age.

Since then there has been remarkably little rebuilding in the centre of Henley, which has never been disembowelled in the interests of progress, as has happened in varying degrees in Maidenhead, Reading and High Wycombe, for instance. It is in large measure because Henley had been deprived in the 1840's of its most important commercial functions, that the town has managed to retain much of the beauty of the pre-industrial age. This has given a cachet to its new role as a primarily residential town, the predominantly service industries of which have in the course of time generated a new economic life of their own.

But although many of the buildings to be seen in these photographs still stand, the traffic in the streets, and on the river too, has changed almost beyond recognition, thanks to the motor car and the motor launch. Even in 1930 (the terminal date for the photographs reproduced here) the motor had hardly begun to exert its baneful influence, and the absence of the motor car from almost all the following photographs provides the single most striking visual contrast between the Henley of fifty years ago and of today.

Acknowledgments

I am much indebted to the following for permission to reproduce photographs in their collections: George Bushell and Son, nos. 1, 6-11, 22, 24, 27, 32, 34-36, 49, 52, 54, 64-66, 68-76; Richard Way, Booksellers, nos. 2, 3, 16, 17, 21, 23, 25, 29-31, 33, 51, 60-62; Mr. C.E. Leaver, nos. 4, 20, 63, 67; Miss Sybil Reeves, nos. 5, 12-15, 37-42, 45, 55; W.H. Brakspear and Sons P.C.L., nos. 57-59; Oxfordshire County Libraries, nos. 19, 44, 46-48, 50, 56.

I am also most grateful to the following for valuable help in various ways: Gary Broad, Diana Cook, Miss Sybil Reeves, Joanna Sheppard, and Messrs. Brian Bushell, John Crocker, Bert Hammant, C.E. Leaver, Gordon Mintern, Michael Shemilt and A.E. Smith.

1. Henley from the south-east in about 1870. With the advent of motor launches the river has changed more than the buildings in this scene of idyllic tranquillity.

2. Henley from the air in the 1920's. Most of the long narrow gardens on either side of Hart Street were then still unbuilt upon. King's Road (at the top left) was a cul-de-sac ending in fields, and the Mount View, Abrahams and Baronsmead estates, and the car park, were all things of the future. In the foreground, to the right of the railway station, can be seen the circular turntable on which the larger steam locomotives had to be revolved before returning to Twyford.

HENLEY REGATTA: GRAND STAND AND PHYLLIS COURT CLUB

3. Part of the Regatta course, seen from the air in the 1920's. The four-day Regatta, held every year at the beginning of July, attracts competitors from all over the world. This photograph shows large numbers of boats crowded beside the booms which are put up every year to keep the course clear. In the centre of the picture is the floating grandstand, with the finishing post beside it; and to its left are the main grandstand and the refreshment tents in the Regatta Stewards' Enclosure. Behind the Enclosure is the fair, which until the Stewards decided in about 1968 to use this piece of land as a car park, was a very popular adjunct of the Regatta. To the right of the fair are the boat tents, and at bottom right among the trees is Phyllis Court Club.

4. Henley seen from the tower of Friar Park in about 1910. In the foreground are the gardens of Sir Frank Crisp, the creator and owner of Friar Park (see also plates 60-61). Prominent landmarks include (from left to right) the tower of St. Mary's Church, Park Place (visible among the trees on top of the hill), the Town Hall and the tower and spire of the Congregational (now United Reformed) Church, which was built at the expense of Sir Frank Crisp in 1908.

5. Henley from Portobello Hill in about 1890. This photograph was taken from the field which soon afterwards became the site of St. Mark's Road. On the left are Normanstead, Holy Trinity Church and its vicarage. The field in front of them is now the site of Trinity School. The prominent little house to the right is Normanstead Lodge. Behind it and slightly to the right, the three-windowed house is Stoneleigh House, 13 Reading Road. To the right of this and partly hidden by trees, is the old Congregational Chapel.

6. The toll-gate and toll-collector's cottage at the Berkshire end of Henley Bridge. The bridge was built in 1781-1786 under an Act of Parliament which authorized the collection of tolls to pay for the cost (about £10,000). By 1873 the whole amount had been paid off and the tolls were discontinued. This photograph was probably taken in 1868, when the cast-iron lamp columns at the four corners of the bridge were in course of erection. Note in the background the open field and hedgerow trees on the site where Friar Park was later built.

7. The bridge, toll-gate and toll-collector's cottage from Henley, looking towards Remenham. Like the facing picture, this photograph was probably taken in 1868 when the cast-iron lamp columns on the bridge were erected but the glass lamp globes had not yet been put on (see also plate 70). The house in the centre stands upon the site of the present Thamesmead in Remenham Lane. In the background Remenham Hill was much less wooded than it is now.

8. The bridge and Waterside from Lion Meadow in about 1880. On the extreme left is the future site of Leander Club's clubhouse, built in 1896. Behind the bridge is River Terrace, built in 1866, to the left of which is the blank rear wall of the first Royal Hotel, built in 1869 and demolished around 1900 (see plate 42). Behind the Angel on the Bridge is the malthouse of the Greys Brewery in Friday Street. The building with the pedimented archway was the entrance to the Red Lion stable yard. Stables and hay lofts occupied the long two-storey range to the right, rebuilt in about 1890 as the Red Lion boat-house, and now the Century Galleries. The little white house to the right was the Little White Hart before its rebuilding on an extended site in 1900. On the extreme right are the stables of Brakspear's Brewery.

9. Waterside and the corner of New Street and Wharf Lane in the early 1880's, probably during the Regatta. The gabled building on the left housed the stables of Brakspear's Brewery and was later occupied for many years by Henley Rowing Club. Behind the house-boat with the flags are the decayed wharfs and commercial premises of Wharf Lane, all soon afterwards demolished.

10. The river frontage of Wharf Lane, probably in about 1885, before its rebuilding. The three boat-houses on the left seem to be built of wood, and were probably the short-lived precursors of the present brick boat-houses there. Most of the waterside was still occupied by timber merchants and barge builders. The little house with two windows in front of the large tree in the centre was the Ship inn in Wharf Lane. At the extreme left are the two chimneys of Brakspear's Brewery, whose great malthouse on the north side of New Street (see plate 59) was later built in the centre background of this photograph.

11. The rest of the river frontage of Wharf Lane, probably in about 1885, during the Regatta. This site is now occupied by Wharfe House, Magdalen House and Manor Garden.

701. Henley Royal Regatta, 1881, The Finish.

12. Henley Royal Regatta, the finish of a race in 1881, seen from the bridge. The Henley Reach is the longest stretch of straight water on the whole of the on-tidal Thames. Henley Regatta was established here in 1839, and until 1885 the finishing post was within a few yards of Henley Bridge. The best vantage points for spectators were along Waterside between New Street and the bridge, and along the towing path in Lion Meadow (to the right). The course was not piled or boomed, and three crews competed in each race, as in this photograph.

13. Henley Bridge during the Regatta, view from upstream in the early 1880's. When the finishing post was so near, the bridge was another popular vantage point, while on the water skiffs were by far the commonest craft.

14. Until 1885 the Regatta grandstand was put up in the roadway of Waterside in front of the Red Lion stables. This photograph was taken in the early 1880's and shows the grandstand and (to the left) the judges' pavilion. At the extreme right is the Little White Hart.

15. Another view of the Regatta grandstand in the early 1880's. The steam pinnace in the foreground was probably the umpires' launch. In the background are the obsolescent buildings of Wharf Lane, already hemmed in by house-boats and pleasure craft and soon afterwards demolished. The three boat-houses on the right, with gables and balconies, are the same as those shown on plate 10, and were evidently the precursors of the present brick boat-houses there.

Royal Regatta, Henley-on-Thames

16. In 1886 the finishing point of the Regatta course was moved about three hundred yards down-stream, thereby eliminating the bend in the river near the end of the old course. At the same time the course was piled and boomed in order to keep the ever-increasing numbers of skiffs and punts clear of the competitors' water; and the number of crews in each race was reduced from three to two. This photograph, taken in about 1905, shows the finish of a race along the new course. The judges' stand is on the right, and the umpires' steam or electric launch is in the background.

THE RIVER LOOKING TO THE BRIDGE, HENLEY.

17. The Regatta reached its zenith in Edwardian times, and this photograph, taken in about 1905, shows the river crowded with spectators' boats after the conclusion of racing. It was taken from nearly the same spot as plate 8, but by 1905 the Red Lion's old stables had been replaced by a new boat-house, the Little White Hart (in the centre, with three steep gables) had been enlarged and rebuilt in 1900, and in Wharf Lane great new boat-houses (to the right) had succeeded the now out-of-date commercial buildings there.

18. Spectators on a house-boat moored on the Buckinghamshire side of the river in about 1900. At this time the Regatta was held on three consecutive days in the middle of the week, and the idea of having it on a Saturday or Sunday, as now, had not even been contemplated. It was therefore primarily a sporting and social occasion for people of leisure and means, managed (as it still is today) in an entirely paternalistic way by some fifty private gentlemen known as the Stewards. Admittance to the social sanctuary of the Stewards' own Enclosure near the finishing point on the Berkshire side is still strictly regulated, and anyone whose dress does not comply with the Stewards' rigorous precepts is refused entry.

19. House-boats moored off Fawley Meadows in the 1890's. The Stewards now own much land on both sides of the Regatta course, including Fawley Meadows. Today there are no longer any house-boats, and nearly all visitors come to the Regatta by car. In recent years they have come in ever-increasing numbers, providing the Stewards in 1982 with an income of over half a million pounds, from which the ever-rising costs of the Regatta are paid.

318. A BIT OF OLD HENLEY.

20. The Market Place, Town Hall, Gravel Hill and West Hill in about 1880. Until nearly the end of the eighteenth century a narrow range of buildings known as Middle Row extended down the centre of the Market Place and part of Hart Street. Soon after the building of Henley Bridge in 1781-1786 all of Middle Row was demolished in order to improve the access to and from the bridge. The buildings taken down included the Market House, Guildhall and the town gaol, which were replaced in 1795-1796 by a new Town Hall, built and designed by William Bradshaw, an Alderman of Henley Corporation. The obelisk at the cross was put up in the 1780's as a milestone, three of its sides being inscribed with the distances to Reading, Oxford and London. It remained here until 1885. (See also plates 27 and 50.)

21. The present Town Hall was built in 1899-1901 to commemorate the Diamond Jubilee of Queen Victoria. The architect was Henry T. Hare and the builder McCarthy E. Fitt. The wrought-iron gates at the main entrance were removed many years ago, and are now at Holy Trinity Church. At the extreme left of the picture, behind the little white house, is the brewery of Ives Brothers, a small firm of family brewers with its own malthouse at the rear, now St. Mary's Hall.

22. The old Town Hall from the rear in about 1860. This photograph shows the Town Hall as originally built, the main body of it being supported on sixteen stone columns, and the open space beneath being used for the transaction of business by 'the corn dealers, farmers and other gentlemen who are in the habit of attending the Market'. On the extreme right is the sign of the Cannon inn, now a restaurant.

THE MARKET PLACE. HENLEY.

23. The new Town Hall from the rear, probably during the Regatta in about 1905. On the right, next to the Cannon, is the Broad Gates, now occupied by and partly rebuilt by Stuart Turner's, the famous firm of pump manufacturers. The Broad Gates was one of the oldest and most picturesque inns in Henley, much favoured by farmers on market days. At the rear there was a 'Great Room' where plays were sometimes performed by touring companies of actors. One such visit was made in 1798 by the actor-managers Sampson Penley and John Jonas, who later provided themselves with a permanent home in Henley by building the Kenton Theatre in New Street.

24. In 1870 the Henley Corporation enclosed the open piazza beneath the Town Hall, and enlarged the floor area by the addition of a single-storey pill-box and lean-to on either side. This photograph was taken soon afterwards, evidently in bad weather, to judge frome the filthy state of the road. Behind the Town Hall may be seen the Greyhound inn (later rebuilt as the Victoria), and behind the man beside the cart, the side entrance to the Henley Fire Brigade Station.

THE CRAZIES   CRAZIES HILL

25. When the old Town Hall was about to be demolished in 1899, Alderman Charles Clements bought it and re-erected it (in slightly modified form) as a private house at Crazies Hill, where it still stands and is called The Crazies. Alderman Clements was a builder by trade, employing over a hundred men, and was six times Mayor of Henley. He was a Congregationalist and a great Liberal, and as an active supporter of the temperance movement he advocated the immediate closure of all but twelve of Henley's fifty-three pubs.

26. The Market Place and Hart Street in about 1880, as seen from near the Town Hall. Despite the lapse of over a hundred years only about half a dozen of the buildings shown in this photograph have been demolished. Far greater changes have occurred in the roadway, where the quiet and stillness of this Victorian scene have been destroyed by the rush and roar of the motorised twentieth century.

27. Hart Street from the cross in about 1895. Barclay's Bank Chambers, the large out-of-scale building in the centre, is one of the few new-comers in this range. It was built in 1892 by the London and County Bank; the architect was W. Campbell Jones and the contractor was J. Weyman. The building partly visible on the extreme right, at the corner of Duke Street, was originally the Henley Restaurant, built and opened in 1893. Further down the street, a proposal in the 1930's to demolish the handsome eighteenth-century brick house (to the left of the man with the bicycle, now 18 Hart Street) and put up a cinema there was narrowly averted after loud local protest. The drinking fountain in the right foreground stood at the cross from 1885 to 1903. (See also plate 35.)

28. Hart Street on market day in the late 1880's. The two carriages in the left foreground plied for hire for passengers, but all the others look as if they had been driven in from the country, perhaps for some special occasion. The scores of horses needed to move all these vehicles were presumably stabled at the adjacent inns. The workaday dress of the pedestrians contrasts sharply with the finery worn by spectators at the Regatta (see plate 18).

29. Hart Street in about 1905, view towards St. Mary's Church. At this time the two brick private houses on the left (with the ladder leaning against them) had not yet been incorporated into the Catherine Wheel, where the sign over the entrance proclaims 'Good Stabling and Motor Accommodation'.

30. Hart Street, here seen in a view of about 1910 looking towards the Town Hall, was not 'planned', and it has no individual buildings of outstanding quality. Nevertheless (to quote Robert Herrick's lines) it has a 'sweet disorder' which is more pleasing 'than when Art is too precise in every part'. On the left 'Booth's Motor Repair Works and Garage' at 34 and 36 Hart Street (now a ladies' shoe boutique) sold 'Carburine Motor Spirit'. The very shallow gutters on either side of the road were intended for the needs of horse-drawn traffic, but were not so well suited for motors, one of which may be seen parked on the right in the middle distance.

31. The Market Place and Hart Street in about 1900. The tall building partly visible on the extreme left, now the National Westminster Bank, was erected in 1891. To the right of it the shop with the white fascia and a milk churn in front of it housed the Remenham Dairy. The red pillar-box, which still stands on the pavement nearby, must then have been fairly new, as were the street lamps put up by the Borough Council. The gutter on the left has been relaid in the modern fashion, but on the right the wide shallow type still survived when this photograph was taken.

32. The Old White Hart in Hart Street is undoubtedly the flagship of Henley's famous fleet of pubs. It is so old that it has even given its name to the principal street in the town, and despite all the internal alterations made in recent years by its owners, W.H. Brakspear and Sons, several of its rooms, and the galleried yard, still have a timeless quality not to be found in any other pub in Henley. This photograph shows it before the refronting done in 1931, before its name had acquired the prefix 'Old', when 'Stabling' had not yet been displaced by 'Motors', and when the French word 'Garage' was still such a recent importation that the signwriter thought it ought to have a circumflex accent over the second 'a'.

Catharine Wheel Hotel   *Henley-on-Thames*

33. There has been an inn called the Catherine Wheel in Hart Street since at least 1541. The Catherine Wheel is now a non-residential Berni Inn occupying what were originally probably four separate dwellings. On the left of this photograph, taken around 1900, is the original bow-fronted inn, which expanded, in the Catherine Wheel's heyday in the coaching era of the early nineteenth century, into the next-door house. The whole façade was then united by a coat of stucco applied to both houses, with the name (note the spelling) prominently displayed along the inn's whole front. At the rear there was extensive stabling. Some time later the two adjoining private houses (see plate 29) were added to the hotel. In 1961 the then owners' proposal to demolish the whole building and erect a row of little shops with flats above evoked a very strong local protest, and after a public inquiry permission was refused.

34. The Market Place (left), and Bell Street (right) in about 1910. The building occupied by Monk's draper's shop was demolished in the 1950's. Next door to it was the Feathers Hotel (now Spiers' travel agency), later rebuilt in a florid style and ornamented with the Prince of Wales's Feathers in plaster. Then came the Oxford Temperance Hotel (now the Midland Bank site), a teetotal establishment no doubt approved of by Alderman Clements. The adjoining house, occupied by a corn merchant, still stands and is now a Chinese restaurant. Further to the left is the Remenham Dairy, this house having been replaced long ago by the single-storey Co-op shop.

35. The Phillimore Fountain was erected at the cross in 1885 in memory of Greville Phillimore, rector of Henley from 1867 to 1883, and to whom (according to a contemporary obituary) Henley was 'indebted for its schools, its school of art, nursing-home, invalid's kitchen, parochial hall, and other useful institutions'. The fountain was presented to the town by the late rector's family and friends. It was made by James Forsyth of Hampstead, but the steps, plumbing and foundations were by Alderman Clements of Henley. The four lamps, which were removed after only a few years, were by Hodge of Hatton Garden. The fountain took the place of the obelisk, which was removed to Northfield End (see plate 50), but it too obstructed the traffic, and in 1903 the fountain was also removed, its place of exile being at the other end of Hart Street close to the parish church, where it still stands.

36. Duke Street in the 1860's, looking north to the cross. In 1870 the Henley Local Government Board, which then discharged many of the functions performed after 1883 by the Borough Council, decided to widen Duke Street by buying up all the houses on the west side and setting back the line of frontage. This was done shortly afterwards, mainly at the instigation of J.S. Burn, the historian of Henley and a former member of the Board. All the buildings on the west side of Duke Street have been rebuilt since 1870, and most of those on the east side.

37. The Congregational (now United Reformed) Church in Reading Road in course of erection in 1907-1908. There has been a Congregational community in Henley since at least 1662. Its first chapel (on the right) was built in 1719, enlarged in 1829, and demolished shortly after the completion of the present church, the tower and spire of which was paid for by Sir Frank Crisp (see plate 60). The architect of the new church was Hampden W. Pratt, and the builders Walden and Cox. On the extreme left is the old British School, built in 1856, which is now occupied by the Thames Carpet Cleaning Company.

38. Caxton Terrace, Station Road, in 1893. Caxton Terrace was built in 1885, and in 1893 residents there could still look out to open fields. This part of Station Road was originally laid out to only half its present width, but when a second carriageway was formed in 1926, the trees here seen standing on the pavement were left in what became the centre of the road.

39. The branch line from Twyford to Henley was built by the Great Western Railway Company and opened in 1857. This view shows the entrance to Henley station in the early twentieth century. The whole building except the platform canopy was demolished in 1975, and a row of shops was built upon the site soon afterwards. Nearly ten years later Henley still has no proper station.

40. View taken in 1902 from the signal box towards the station, shortly before the erection of the platform canopy. The departing train is the local branch train for Twyford. In the background can be seen the substantial goods shed, the site of which is now occupied by part of the car park, and the newly completed Imperial (now Edwardian) Hotel in Station Road.

41. Another view taken on the same day in 1902 from the signal box, looking south, and showing the arrival of a train. At this time the journey to Paddington on the fastest through train took only fifty minutes, and nearly 100,000 tickets a year were issued at Henley.

42. The first Royal Hotel, seen from Mill Meadows in about 1880. This large building was put up in 1869-1870 at the corner of Station Road and Thameside. It projected some thirty feet in front of the building line of River Terrace (built in 1866), to which it rudely presented its rear. It proved a commercial failure and after most of it had been demolished the second Royal Hotel was built upon the site in 1899-1900, the architect being G.W. Webb of Reading. Most of this was later turned into flats, now known as Royal Mansions. The house on the extreme left was for some years occupied by a convent of Ursuline nuns.

43. Corner of Friday Street and Thameside in about 1885. This old building was used for centuries as a riverside granary and warehouse for goods landed at or exported from Henley by boat. This picture shows it at the nadir of its fortunes, when almost all commercial traffic on the Thames had been killed by the railways, but before such buildings had been converted into desirable 'olde worlde' riverside cottages. It is now known as Barn Cottage and the Old Granary. The cart on the right belonged to C. Barnett and Sons, Hambleden Mills.

44. The north side of Friday Street looking west from near the river in the late 1880's. This is one of the oldest streets in Henley, and this side of it is one of the least changed of them during the past century. Every building in this picture is still standing, though nearly all of them have been much 'done up'.

45. Friday Street looking east towards the river in the late 1880's. All the buildings on the right between the Black Horse (now 16 Friday Street and no longer a pub) and the projecting first-floor window in the background have been demolished, many of them in the 1930's for the Drill Hall. The tall building in the centre was part of the Greys Brewery, which in 1896 was bought and closed by W.H. Brakspear and Sons Ltd.

46. Bell Street from the cross in about 1890. Almost all of the buildings on the west (i.e. left) side between the cross and the Bull inn have been rebuilt during the last fifty years. On the left is the Phillimore fountain (see plate 35) and behind it is Monk's drapery store. The three-storey building next to Monk's was formerly Painter's famous family grocery store until competition from the supermarkets forced it to close in 1967. Further down, No. 17 (now part of Burnell's) was put up in 1887. The rounded corner-house on the right was built in 1812, its frontage being set back to relieve the increasing press of traffic which passed through Henley after the building of the bridge in 1781-1786.

47. Bell Street looking north in about 1895. On the left the house behind the flag was later demolished for the building of the cinema. On the east (or right) side the Duke of Cumberland pub has been renamed Ye Olde Bell, and the house next door but one to it was rebuilt in 1958 by its present owners, Hammants, the old-established family firm of electricians and electrical contractors.

48. Bell Street looking north in about 1895. On the left the shop now occupied by Gladys Falloon was still used as a private house, with railings in front of it. The buildings on the other side of the archway were demolished in 1964-1965 by Waitrose, who were however compelled to retain the façade of the part of their premises now used as their wine store. In the centre background, on the right side of the street, what is now Bell Street Motors was rebuilt in about 1954 after a severe fire.

49. The Picture Palace at 33 Bell Street was originally a roller-skating rink with a corrugated-iron roof. In 1912 this was converted into a cinema, as seen here. In 1937 the whole building was demolished, and after the line of frontage had been set back, the present Regal Cinema was built to the design of L.T. Hunt. It was opened by the Mayor of Henley, Mr. J.E. Chalcraft, on 14 May 1937, and the main film in the first programme was 'Take My Tip', starring Jack Hulbert and Cicely Courtnedge.

50. Northfield End looking south in about 1890. The obelisk, originally a milestone, had stood at the cross (see plate 20) until 1885, when it was removed to Northfield End. It remained here until 1970, when it was taken down because its site was required for a new traffic scheme. It should then have been returned to the centre of the Market Place, near its original site, but after much debate it was eventually re-erected in Mill Meadows, where it still stands, forlorn and irrelevant to its surroundings. In the background is the beautiful early eighteenth-century house known as Countess Gardens.

51. Northfield End looking south in about 1905. Nearly all the buildings in this photograph still stand, but the scene has nevertheless changed greatly in recent years. The great cedar of Lebanon in the centre, whose splendid shape was at the time of this photograph obscured by the surrounding bushes, finally succumbed to the weight of snow on its branches in December 1981. Between Northfield House and Sydney House Hotel are the stone piers of the gate into the garden of Northfield House, now occupied by Baronsmead. At the extreme right is the garage recently demolished for the building of Northfield Court.

52. Leicester House, on the west side of Northfield End, in about 1860. This stucco-faced house was latterly occupied by Sir Osbert Lancaster, the distinguished author and cartoonist. It was demolished in about 1968, when the sixteen Neo-Georgian houses known as Leicester Close were built upon its site and that of its large garden at the back. To the left of Leicester House, in the brick building with a porch, is the Friends' (Quaker) Meeting House, which was rebuilt in 1894. The ditch behind the woman and child is the Assenden Stream, which crossed in a culvert from the east to the west side of the road about a hundred yards further north.

53. Northfield End, looking north, in 1915. On the left are the railings of the garden of Leicester House, and the open course of the Assenden Stream, which was not flowing at the time of this photograph. There were always plenty of public houses in Henley, and in this picture there are three — the white house on the left behind the lamp-post was the Hope inn, and is now a private house. The first little house on the right (with a white front) was also a pub, and the last house on the right, also white, was the Old White Horse. In the 1930's this pub was demolished and the present Old White Horse, set back from the road, was built a few yards to the east. In the background, on the right of the road, is the boundary wall of the Fawley Court estate, built in 1804.

54. The Fairmile, probably in 1875. The avenue of elms is said to have been planted by Sir William Stapleton, Lord of the Manor of Benson, who died in 1740. All the surviving trees were finally cut down in 1953, and a new avenue of Turkey oaks was planted to commemorate the coronation of Queen Elizabeth II. More recently, an inner avenue of limes was added to commemorate the Silver Jubilee of her accession. The wall on the right was built by Strickland Freeman of Fawley Court to mark the boundary of his estate. The Assenden Stream, seen here in full spate, never flowedd regularly, and changes in the water table caused by the boring of artesian wells are said to be the cause of its having hardly run at all in recent years.

55. At the north end of the Fairmile, where the roads to Nettlebed and Stonor divide, there formerly stood a small pub called the Traveller's Rest. This picture was taken in about 1900, when W.H. Brakspear and Sons were building a larger new pub behind the old one, which was demolished shortly afterwards. The architect was W.G. Hambling of Reading. In 1939 this pub was in turn demolished when its site was required for the formation of the dual carriageway up Bix Hill. The name and licence were then transferred to the large newly built Traveller's Rest in Caversham.

56. New Street from the river in the mid-1890's. Brakspear's had not yet built their mineral water factory on the south side of New Street, or the malthouse on the north side. Their horses were still stabled in the building on the extreme left, now the home of Henley Rowing Club. In the background is the newly built tower of Friar Park, which is now concealed by the trees around it.

57. Brakspear's Brewery and mineral water factory, New Street, in about 1900. Brakspear's is one of fewer than a hundred independent breweries still in business, and the quality of its beer is famous all over England. The mineral water factory, on the right, was built in 1897.

58. Brakspear's Brewery yard, New Street, in about 1900. Horse-drawn drays were, and lorries still are, loaded from the bay on the right, and then driven out through the narrow gateway seen in plate 57. The bunches of holly and mistletoe suspended from the projecting eaves bring prosperity to the firm, which recently celebrated its bicentenary.

59. The malthouse, stables and cart sheds at Brakspear's Brewery, New Street, in about 1900. This impressive group of buildings was put up on the north side of New Street in 1899, soon after Brakspear's became a limited company and bought out its only local rival, the Greys Brewery in Friday Street. Brakspear's no longer make their own malt, and the future of the malthouse is uncertain.

338. A Reflection, Friar Park, Henley-on-Thames.

60. Friar Park was built by Sir Frank Crisp (1843-1919), senior partner in a firm of City solicitors specialising in company law. It was a rich man's whimsical folly, designed by its owner (with assistance from M. Clarke Edwards) in a wholly idiosyncratic French Flamboyant Gothic manner. Although himself a Nonconformist, Sir Frank chose friars as the decorative theme for the house, no doubt in allusion to Friar's Field, the old name of the land where the house stood; and leering, ghoulish friars are represented throughout the interior in sculpture, stained glass and even in such details as the electric light switches.

61. Sir Frank Crisp was also a great authority on horticulture and microscopy, and (according to *The Times*) at Friar Park he 'kept one of the finest gardens in England'. So besides such jokey features as caves, underground lakes and a model of the Matterhorn, there were also twenty-five glass-houses, and for the formation of the Alpine garden over seven thousand tons of stone were brought from Yorkshire. The topiary garden seen here was laid out on the plan of the labyrinth at Versailles. In the 1950's and 1960's Friar Park was used as a convent school by the Salesian Siters of St. John Bosco, and some of the more grotesque 'friars' within were hidden from view. The house is now occupied by Mr. George Harrison, the former Beatle, and both it and the gardens have been extensively restored.

62. Phyllis Court Club in about 1910. The clubhouse occupies the site of a mediaeval manor house, but the existing building dates mainly from the mid nineteenth century. It stands in beautiful grounds sloping down to the riverside near the finish of the Regatta course. Phyllis Court Club was founded by Captain Roy Finlay in 1906 during the Edwardian heyday of the Regatta. For spectators not primarily interested in the rowing, afternoon tea on the lawns provided a congenial way of savouring the social scene.

63. Paradise (or Deanfield) House, Gravel Hill, in late Victorian or Edwardian times. It was here that Mary Blandy first met Captain W.H. Cranstoun and formed the attachment which led to her execution for the murder of her father in 1752. This was also the home from 1852 until his death in 1882 of William Brakspear the brewer, four times mayor of Henley. Paradise House was demolished in the late 1960's and the Milton Close housing estate was built on its site and that of its extensive grounds in 1969-1970. On the right of this picture is the garden wall along Gravel Hill, which still stands.

64. Henley Borough Council in session in the old Town Hall in 1895. The Mayor, standing, was Alderman Anker Simmons, partner in the old Henley firm of Simmons and Sons, surveyors. Immediately on his right is Alderman Charles Clements, who subsequently bought the Town Hall and re-erected it at Crazies Hill (see plate 25). Standing beneath the picture is Mr. Savage, the Town Sergeant. The tables and chairs seen in this photograph are still in use in the Committee Room at the present Town Hall, and the very fine silver-gilt mace, made in 1722, is still placed on the table at meetings of the Town Council. The portrait is of George I, by Sir Godfrey Kneller.

65. Henley Volunteer Fire Brigade in about 1900. The Fire Brigade was established in 1868, and its station, where monthly drills took place, was for many years in the Upper Market Place above the Town Hall. The engine seen here is a Merryweather horse-drawn steam 'Firefly', and was the Henley Brigade's first non-manual engine. The studied masculine postures of the firemen, and their grouping round the table, show that this was a very carefully posed photograph.

66. Preparing to lay the foundation stone of the Town Hall in 1899. The ceremony was performed on 9 June 1899 by the Hon. W.F.D. Smith, M.P. (1868-1928), grandson of the founder of the firm of W.H. Smith and Son, and later Viscount Hambleden. Smith's country house was at Greenlands, and he was 'a munificent contributor to the building Fund' for the Town Hall.

67. In August 1914 the Town Hall was converted into a military hospital with twenty-four beds in the large hall. The first patients arrived in October, and were looked after by the Henley Voluntary Aid Detachment, 20 Oxon (Royal Red Cross Society).

68. The Henley postman. This very early photograph was probably taken in the 1850's.

69. John Moss (extreme left, with top hat), agricultural machine maker of Northfield End, and his men in the 1850's. The man on the right was probably the foreman. The device on the left is a tyring machine for wooden cartwheels, in the centre is a potato seeder, and on the right is a swede masher.

70. In 1900 the population of Henley was still under 6,000, and the everyday life of the townspeople was much more closely related to the workaday life of the surrounding country than it is now. So this series of photographs ends with a few pictures of the country, the river and riverside buildings. Here is the bridge and Lion Meadow, perhaps in the 1880's. The cast-iron lamp-standard on the right and three others at each corner of the bridge, were put up in 1868. The last of the newly planted poplars seen here, the one at the bend of the river known as Poplar Point, was cut down in 1983.

71. In recent years the Thames Conservancy and the Thames Water Authority have been able to keep effective control over the river when in spate, and so floods in Henley are now almost unknown. But on 12 March 1774 the old wooden bridge had been actually 'carried away'. The new stone bridge withstood its first great test on 28 January 1809, when the waters rose to the level recorded on a stone let into the wall of the Red Lion, and another in November 1894, when this photograph was probably taken. Over the years some subsidence had, however, taken place in the two piers at the Henley end of the bridge (as the kink in the parapet here shows), where the force of the current is strongest, and in 1906-1907 a diver placed over five hundred tons of concrete and cement in bags around the abutments.

72. The Two Brewers pub, Wargrave Road, under water, probably in the flood of November 1894.

73. Floods in New Street, probably in November 1894. The fine house on the left, 55 New Street, was built in about 1715, this being the date incised on a brick beside the ground-floor window on the left. The hood over the doorway was unfortunately removed some years ago, and an unsuitable modern one put up in its place.

74. Climatic changes may explain why the Thames seldom freezes nowadays, and certainly not hard enough to permit the skating seen here, perhaps during the winter of 1909-1910.

75. The Henley Reach of the river in late Victorian times, looking towards Temple Island. The temple was designed by James Wyatt in 1771 for Sambrooke Freeman of Fawley Court. On the left is the Fawley Court boat-house, a few remains of which still survive, now surrounded by trees.

76. Haymaking near Hambleden, some two and a half miles from Henley, in the 1890's. This field was part of the Greenlands estate purchased in 1871 by W.H. Smith, M.P., son of the founder of the famous business. The identity of the two gentlemen on horseback on the left of this carefully posed photograph has not been discovered. The two women in the foreground look a little too well dressed to be real haymakers.